Invitation to BALLET

A Celebration of Dance and Degas

By Carolyn Vaughan

Works of art by Edgar Degas

Illustrations by Rachel Isadora

THE METROPOLITAN MUSEUM OF ART

ABRAMS BOOKS FOR YOUNG READERS

New York

Introduction

Balancing on tiptoe, leaping across the stage, stretching their arms and legs into beautiful arabesques—ballet dancers look as though they are floating like feathers or flying like fairies. But becoming a ballerina is hard work. Ballet dancers take classes and practice for years to train their bodies and learn the many steps and leaps. This book is an invitation to ballet. Here, you'll find out what happens in ballet class, learn about some of the steps, and discover what makes being a ballet dancer so special.

Edgar Degas, a French artist of the late nineteenth and early twentieth centuries, was fascinated by the ballet. He went to classes, rehearsals, and performances at the Paris Opéra, a ballet school and company. Degas made hundreds of paintings, drawings, prints, and sculptures of the dancers. Some of his works are reproduced in *Invitation to Ballet*.

Degas once said about drawing, "One must repeat the same subject ten times, a hundred times. Nothing in art must seem an accident, not even movement." It's the same with ballet. A dancer must repeat the same movement a hundred times, a thousand times, until each step is perfect.

Edgar Degas helped launch the Impressionist art movement in the late nineteenth century. Impressionist artists had different styles, but their works often featured loose brushwork, unblended colors, and unusual viewpoints or cropping, such as in this painting. Instead of placing his main subject—the ballerina—in the center, Degas has positioned her to the side.

Getting Ready to Dance

When you go to ballet class, wear clothes that allow you to move freely. Girls wear tights and a leotard. Tutus are for special occasions, like performances, but sometimes you can wear a practice tutu or a ballet skirt to class. Boys can wear a T-shirt with shorts or tights. These clothes will also let your teacher see that your positions and movements are correct.

Your ballet slippers should fit very well. An elastic strap will help to keep them in place. Tie the drawstrings in a bow and tuck them inside your shoes.

Always keep your hair neat and tidy. A bun shows off your neck and shoulders and gives your body a graceful line from head to toe. If you have short hair, wear a headband to keep your hair out of your eyes.

It's best not to wear jewelry to class because it could scratch someone or get caught in your clothes.

A GOOD POINT
Dancing *en pointe* (on the tips of the toes) makes ballerinas look weightless, like the fairies, sprites, and swans they often play. But their muscles and bones have to be very strong. Ballet students don't start wearing toe shoes until they are at least eleven years old and have taken several years of classes.

One dancer adjusts her tutu while, behind her, another dancer fixes her hair in Edgar Degas's picture. The colored sashes and ribbons worn by Degas's dancers add a touch of brightness and bring his works of art to life.

The Ballet Class

Ballet classes are taught in a studio that is designed just for ballet. The floor is specially built to allow for softer landings. There are mirrors on the walls so you can check your position. A wooden handrail called a barre runs along the wall. You'll hold—lightly—on to the barre to do some of the exercises and positions.

One of the first things you'll learn is how to stand like a ballet dancer, with your back straight (but not stiff), your stomach pulled in, and your tailbone dropped down. Your rib cage should be in line with your hips, your shoulders relaxed, and the top of your head lifted toward the ceiling.

Your ballet classes may begin with some simple stretches, either on the floor or standing up. It's important to do all the stretches so that your muscles are warmed up and ready to dance.

A side split stretches the legs and back.

After that, most classes have three parts: exercises at the barre, more practice in the center, then jumps and traveling steps. But first, you have to know where ballet starts—with the five positions.

Most dancing is done to music. Some classes have a pianist, and others use recorded music. In Edgar Degas's time, a violinist sometimes played for classes.

The Five Positions

*A*ll ballet steps begin and end in one of five basic positions. They are the same positions that dancers have been using for more than three hundred years!

In ballet, every movement is done with the legs "turned out" from the hip and the toes pointing away from each other. Turnout allows you to change the position of your feet and move in any direction very quickly. It also makes your legs look longer.

First position

Second position

Third position

Fourth position

Fifth position

THE LITTLE FOURTEEN-YEAR-OLD DANCER

The girl who posed for Edgar Degas's sculpture was named Marie van Goethem. She was a student and then a dancer in the Paris Opéra ballet company. She modeled for Degas many times. Look at the way she is standing. Even though her feet are in fourth position, she is leaning back a little, not in ballet posture ready to dance. Maybe she's taking a break, watching her teacher demonstrate the next step.

At the Barre

Holding lightly on to the barre will help you balance while you learn and practice ballet steps. It will also help you keep your posture and placement. Exercises at the barre start with *pliés* (plee-AYZ), which stretch and strengthen all the leg muscles.

PLIÉ There are two kinds of pliés. In *demi-plié* (duh-MEE-plee-AY), the knees bend halfway. In *grand plié* (grahn plee-AY), the legs bend until the thighs are horizontal. You can do pliés in all five positions, but beginners may start with first, second, and third.

Demi-plié

RELEVÉ Pliés go down, *relevés* (ruhl-VAYZ) go up. In a relevé, you lift up your heels and stand on the balls of your feet and toes. When you begin wearing pointe shoes, you'll rise to the tips of your toes.

BATTEMENTS *Battement tendu* (bat-MAHN tahn-DEW) is usually just called *tendu*, which means "stretched." Without moving your hips, you slide one foot out as far as it will go with the toe pointed and on the floor. Then you slide it back to the beginning position.

Battement tendu

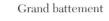
Grand battement

In a *battement dégagé* (day-gah-ZHAY), you briskly brush your foot a couple of inches off the floor before returning to the starting position. In a *grand battement,* you move your leg up higher.

These dancers are doing a leg stretch at the barre. The watering can looks as if it's trying to stretch, too. In Edgar Degas's time, watering cans were kept in the studio to dampen the floor and keep the dust down.

Letting Go

*N*ext, you'll practice some steps without holding on to the barre. At first, you may repeat some pliés, relevés, tendus, and other steps. As you advance, you'll try some slow movements and balance.

ROND DE JAMBE In a *rond de jambe* (rawn duh zhahnb) you make a half circle with your leg (*jambe*). Your foot slides forward, as in a tendu. Then it sketches a semicircle and finally returns to first position. If you had chalk in your slipper, you would have drawn the letter D.

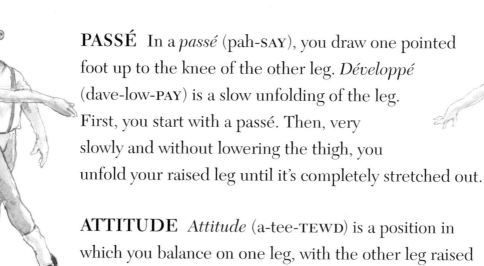

PASSÉ In a *passé* (pah-SAY), you draw one pointed foot up to the knee of the other leg. *Développé* (dave-low-PAY) is a slow unfolding of the leg. First, you start with a passé. Then, very slowly and without lowering the thigh, you unfold your raised leg until it's completely stretched out.

ATTITUDE *Attitude* (a-tee-TEWD) is a position in which you balance on one leg, with the other leg raised to the front, side, or back, and the knee bent.

Rond de jambe

Passé en pointe

A GOOD POINT

In ballet, slow movements are called *adage* (ah-DAHZH). This is the French word for the Italian *adagio*, a musical term meaning "slow." Fast work, such as jumps and traveling steps, is known as *allegro* (ah-LAY-grow), the Italian word for "happy." In music, allegro means "lively" or "brisk."

The ballet master, leaning on his cane, watches as a dancer performs an attitude en pointe in Edgar Degas's painting *The Dance Class*.

Making the Leap

The jumps and traveling steps known as allegro will come next. *Sauter* (so-TAY) means "to jump." Jumps always start and end in a demi-plié, to give you a good bounce and a soft—and safe—landing. Jumps are practiced at the barre, in the center, and traveling across the room.

SAUTÉ A simple sauté is jumping straight up and landing with your feet in the same position. To do an *échappé sauté* (ay-sha-PAY so-TAY), you jump straight up, then open out your feet to land in second or fourth position. Then you jump back to the position you started in.

Grand jeté

CHANGEMENT

Changement (shahnzh-MAHN) is when you jump from third or fifth position and move your feet in the air so that the foot that started out in front ends up in back.

Changement

JETÉS *Jetés* (zhuh-TAYZ) are jumps that start on one foot and end on the other. The *grand jeté* is a more advanced jump. In it, you extend your legs in a full split while in the air and then land on one foot. When you are suspended at the top of the jump, it looks as if you are flying!

PAS DE CHAT The *pas de chat* (pah duh shah), or "cat's step," is like the quick, light leap of a cat. As you jump, you raise first one leg, then the other, then land on one leg with the other quickly following. In the air, your legs are turned out in a diamond shape.

Pas de chat

Whenever a ballet dancer's foot leaves the floor, it is stretched long with the toes pointed. In Edgar Degas's painting, one of the resting dancers even points her toe while adjusting her tights.

Time to Dance

*W*hen you've had a lot of practice and mastered the basics, it will be time to move on to some harder steps and jumps—the ones that every dancer wants to try.

PIROUETTE The *pirouette* (peer-WET) is probably the best-known turning step in ballet. Balancing on one foot with the other foot raised, usually to the knee or ankle, you spin around and around. Sometimes a dancer whips one leg out and back each time she makes a turn. This is called a *fouetté* (fweh-TAY). In the ballet *Swan Lake*, Odile performs thirty-two fouettés!

Arabesque

ARABESQUE The most graceful pose in ballet may be the *arabesque* (a-ra-BESK), in which you balance on one leg with the other extended behind you. Your arms are held in one of several positions that make a long, long line from fingertip to pointed toe.

ENCHAÎNEMENT An *enchaînement* (ahn-shen-MAHN) is a series of steps linked together like a chain. In class, it's also known as a combination. When you link together several enchaînements, you have a dance.

Enchaînement

In this painting, Edgar Degas shows that dancing isn't done just with the feet. In class, you'll learn *port de bras* (pore duh brah), how to hold and move your arms gracefully. You'll also learn to coordinate your eye and head movements with your arms.

A GOOD POINT

Have you ever wondered how a dancer keeps from getting dizzy as she spins around? When she begins a turn, she fixes her eyes straight ahead on a real or imaginary point. As she turns, she keeps looking at that point as long as she can. Then she quickly whips her head around and finds the same spot as she finishes the turn. This is called spotting.

Toe Shoes and Tutus

*I*magine balancing your whole body while standing on an area the size of a half-dollar. That's what it's like to dance in toe shoes. And while pink satin toe shoes look delicate, they are sturdily built. The shank, a piece of stiff material in the sole, gives support to the arch of the foot. The block, the hard box that supports the toes, is made with many layers of fabric or paper held together with glue.

New toe shoes are very stiff, so dancers have to break them in. Some hit the block with a hammer or even close their shoes in a door! Dancers always sew the elastics and ribbons on their shoes themselves. A ballerina in a leading role may wear out one or more pairs of toe shoes in just one performance.

Tutus are the traditional costume for a female dancer. The bell-shaped skirt of the romantic tutu falls to mid-calf. It's made of several layers of soft, filmy tulle. The attached top, or bodice, is usually simple and sleeveless or with very short sleeves.

The short saucer-shaped skirt of the classical tutu shows off the dancer's long legs and dazzling technique. The many layers of stiff mesh fabric make the skirt stand out from the dancer's body. The bodice is usually sleeveless and close-fitting. The whole costume is often decorated with sequins or beads that sparkle under the spotlights.

This dancer is wearing a practice tutu.

A GOOD POINT
A ballet company's tutus are stored upside down to keep them fluffy.

COSTUME CHANGE

Early ballet costumes were bulky and hard to dance in. In the 1700s, Marie Sallé, a dancer and choreographer, changed that. For her role in *Pygmalion*, she wore a simple, flowing robe so she could move more freely. Her rival, Marie Camargo, shortened her skirt to show off her skill at performing difficult steps. In the 1800s, Marie Taglioni became one of the first ballerinas to dance en pointe. Her shoes were modified evening slippers and didn't have a block in the toes. Taglioni was also the first to wear a romantic tutu for her role as a fairylike creature in *La Sylphide* (at right).

The Performance

When they're learning new dances created by the choreographer, dancers sometimes mark, or practice, the steps with their fingers instead of their feet. Edgar Degas's dancer has lifted her tutu over the back of the chair so it won't get rumpled.

*A*t the end of each year of ballet classes, students may dance in a recital. For professional dancers, the work they do, day in and day out, in classes and rehearsals, leads to a performance in a ballet. The ballet master or mistress in charge of the daily class for the company also leads rehearsals for the performances.

The choreographer chooses the subject and the music for a ballet. Then he or she puts together a series of steps to make the dances. The dancers learn the steps in rehearsals and then practice the dances over and over.

Set designers create a whole magical world, whether it's the overgrown castle of *The Sleeping Beauty* or Clara's living room in *The Nutcracker*. The costumes give you a hint about the character the dancer is portraying.

A GOOD POINT

In classic story ballets, such as *Swan Lake* and *The Sleeping Beauty*, dancers use mime to tell the story. In mime, the dancers replace words with gestures or movements. Some gestures have become standard in ballet. For instance, a dancer resting her head on her hands means "sleep."

Although Edgar Degas showed several dancers, he composed this picture to focus on only one ballerina.

Dances for One, Two, Four . . . or a Corps

When one person performs a dance, it's called a solo, or variation. Some variations are performed by the lead dancers, or principals, in a ballet company. An example is the waltz of the Sugar Plum Fairy in *The Nutcracker*. Other solos are part of smaller but still important roles, such as the dance of the Lilac Fairy in *The Sleeping Beauty*.

The *pas de deux* (pah duh deuh), or "step for two," is a dance for two people, usually one woman and one man. A grand pas de deux is made up of several dances. Some may be performed by one of the dancers and others by both performers together. The grand pas de deux is often the centerpiece of a full-length ballet.

A dance for three performers is called a *pas de trois* (trwah) and for four performers, a *pas de quatre* (KA-truh). A favorite pas de quatre is the dance of the little swans in *Swan Lake*. Four dancers perform a series of tricky steps called a petit allegro with their arms linked. Their timing has to be perfect or they might all fall over!

Pas de deux

THE NUTCRACKER (1892)

MUSIC BY PYOTR ILYICH TCHAIKOVSKY
CHOREOGRAPHY BY LEV IVANOV

At a Christmas Eve party, Clara is given a toy nutcracker by her godfather, Herr Drosselmeyer. After the party, she falls asleep, and when she wakes, the toys have come to life. The Nutcracker leads toy soldiers to victory against an army of rats. Then he becomes a prince and sweeps Clara off to the Land of Sweets, where she meets the Sugar Plum Fairy, and dances from around the world are performed for her amusement.

The Rat King

Edgar Degas painted only a few pictures of actual performances. *The Rehearsal Onstage* shows a divertissement from the opera *Don Giovanni,* written in 1787 by Wolfgang Amadeus Mozart.

The Story of Ballet

Ballet traces its roots to Italy and to the courts of kings and dukes in the 1400s and 1500s. The word *ballet* is a French form of the Italian word *ballare*, "to dance." To mark special occasions, such as weddings, the courts presented extravagant pageants that featured dancing. In 1533, when the Italian Catherine de Médicis married the future French king Henry II, she took these elaborate shows to France.

Louis XIV of France loved these court entertainments. In the 1600s, he founded the Académie Royale de la Danse, a professional school of ballet. Its first director, Pierre Beauchamp, made turnout and the five positions the cornerstones of ballet.

When he was just fifteen, Louis XIV appeared in *Le Ballet de la Nuit*, a court entertainment. He played a character called the Sun King, which became his nickname.

In the late 1800s, a Frenchman named Marius Petipa became head of the Imperial Ballet in St. Petersburg, and Russia took center stage in the world of ballet. Petipa choreographed some of the great classic ballets, such as *Swan Lake* and *The Sleeping Beauty*. Anna Pavlova and Tamara Karsavina were two of the famous Russian ballerinas of the time.

Another Russian, Serge Diaghilev, had a great talent for bringing together musicians, choreographers, painters, and dancers. In the early 1900s, he asked artists such as Pablo Picasso and Natalia Goncharova to design sets and costumes. His company toured the world, presenting ballets that were new, different, and sometimes shocking. Vaslav Nijinsky, one of the greatest male dancers of all time, appeared in some of his ballets.

George Balanchine, dancer and choreographer, founded a ballet school and company in New York City. Instead of telling stories, many of his ballets were about just music and dancing.

The Russian artist Léon Bakst created this costume design for Vaslav Nijinksy's role of Iksender in the ballet *La Péri*.

Now, ballet is free to go in many directions, whether cutting-edge modern pieces or old-fashioned fairy-tale fantasies. What hasn't changed about ballet, since the time Edgar Degas was painting it, is the way it sweeps the audience into the mysterious and wondrous world of the imagination.

Degas and the Ballet

Edgar Degas painted this self-portrait about 1854, the year he decided to devote himself to art.

Edgar Degas was born in Paris on July 19, 1834. His father was a wealthy banker who wanted his son to choose a career like banking or law. But Degas was determined to blaze his own trail and declared that he wanted to be a painter.

Though Degas attended art school, he also learned from copying famous paintings in the museums of Paris. Soon he began painting pictures of city life and ordinary people. He painted laundry women and shop girls, cafés and horse races. But his favorite subject would become ballet dancers. In all, Degas made about fifteen hundred works featuring dancers.

Degas spent untold hours behind the scenes at the Paris Opéra, watching the dancers perfect their steps. At first, he had to learn the names and shapes of ballet positions, just as the youngest dancers did. But he soon learned the steps and could even demonstrate them in his studio. And all the time, he was sketching the dancers' slightest movements—even the way a dancer scratched her back!

THE LITTLE RATS

The youngest dancers at the Paris Opéra were affectionately known as *les petits rats*, "the little rats." They got this nickname because they were always scurrying from one place to another, and they were always hungry. The petits rats started their ballet training when they were seven or eight years old. At about fourteen, if they passed an examination, they became members of the corps de ballet.

Unlike other Impressionist artists, Degas did not paint directly and quickly. Instead, he made sketches of dancers as they practiced at the Opéra or modeled for him in his studio. Then he used and reused those drawings in different combinations to make his paintings.

Dancing is an art of movement. But Degas, who watched and learned, who sketched and remembered, gave us still pictures that capture the spirit of ballet and make us see it as it really is.

This ballet slipper was once owned by Edgar Degas.

Unless otherwise noted, the works of art in this book are by Edgar Degas (French, 1834–1917) and are in the collection of The Metropolitan Museum of Art.

PAGE 27
*Costume Study for Nijinsky in the role of Iksender
in the ballet* La Péri
Léon Bakst, Russian, 1866–1924
Watercolor and gold and silver paints over graphite,
26⅝ x 19¼ in., 1922
Gift of Sir Joseph Duveen, 1922   22.226.1

PAGE 28 (TOP)
Self-Portrait (detail)
Oil on paper laid down on canvas, 16 x 13½ in., ca. 1854
Bequest of Stephen C. Clark, 1960   61.101.6

PAGE 28 (BOTTOM)
Dancer, viewed from the right (detail)
Charcoal with white highlights on
rose-beige paper, ca. 1873–74
Musée du Louvre, Paris, Collection fonds Orsay
Photograph: Michele Bellot / © Réunion des Musées Nationaux /
Art Resource, New York

PAGE 29 (TOP)
Little Girl Practicing at the Barre
Black chalk and graphite, heightened with white chalk on pink laid
paper, 12³⁄₁₆ x 11⁹⁄₁₆ in., ca. 1878–80
H. O. Havemeyer Collection, Bequest of Mrs. H. O. Havemeyer,
1929   29.100.943

PAGE 29 (BOTTOM)
Pink satin ballet slipper, once owned by Edgar Degas
Musée d'Orsay, Paris
Photograph: © Réunion des Musées Nationaux / Art Resource,
New York

PAGE 32
Dancer Onstage (detail)
Pastel and gouache on paper, 28⅜ x 30½ in., 1878
Musée d'Orsay, Paris
Photograph: © Erich Lessing / Art Resource, New York

INDEX

Note: Page numbers in *italics* refer to illustrations.

At the end of a performance, the ballerina performs a curtsey called a *révérence* (ray-vay-RAHNS) to the audience to thank them for their applause. At the end of a ballet class, the students do a révérence to show their gratitude to and respect for their teacher.

Library of Congress Cataloging-in-Publication Data

Vaughan, Carolyn.
Invitation to ballet / by Carolyn Vaughan ; works of art by Edgar Degas ; illustrated by Rachel Isadora.
p. cm.
ISBN 978-1-58839-417-0 (MMA)—
ISBN 978-1-4197-0260-0 (Abrams)
1. Ballet—Juvenile literature. 2 Ballet in art—Juvenile literature. 3. Degas, Edgar, 1834-1917—
Juvenile literature. I. Isadora, Rachel, ill. II. Title
GV 1787.5.V38 2011
20110109046

Manufactured in China 0312 SCP Dongguan, Guangdong, PRC
10 9 8 7 6 5 4 3 2 1

Produced by the Department of Special Publications, The Metropolitan Museum of Art: Robie Rogge, Publishing Manager; Linda C. Falken, Senior Editor; Atif Toor, Designer; Mary Wong, Production. Photographs of works of art in the collection of The Metropolitan Museum of Art by The Metropolitan Museum of Art Photograph Studio.

To learn more about Edgar Degas and Impressionism, visit the Department of European Paintings and the Heilbrunn Timeline of Art History on the Museum's website: www.metmuseum.org.

The Metropolitan Museum of Art
1000 Fifth Avenue, New York, NY 10028
212.570.3894
www.metmuseum.org

ABRAMS
THE ART OF BOOKS SINCE 1949
115 West 18th Street
New York, NY 10011
www.abramsbooks.com